Help! The Speaker Can't Come

– BARBARA SOWOOD –

An environmentally friendly book printed and bound in England by
www.printondemand-worldwide.com

Mixed Sources
Product group from well-managed forests, and other controlled sources
www.fsc.org Cert no. TT-COC-002641
© 1996 Forest Stewardship Council

PEFC Certified
This product is from sustainably managed forests and controlled sources
www.pefc.org

This book is made entirely of chain-of-custody materials

www.fast-print.net/store.php

HELP! THE SPEAKER CAN'T COME

A catalogue record for this book is available from the British Library

ISBN 978-178456-175-8

First published 2015 by
FASTPRINT PUBLISHING
Peterborough, England.

DEDICATION

To my friends in the Mothers' Union

ACKNOWLEDGMENTS

Grateful thanks to my daughter, Chris Owen, who meticulously proof-read this book, and to my granddaughter, Ceridwen Williams, who designed the front cover.

CONTENTS

PLAYS

THREE CHRISTMAS MONOLOGUES – The night that changed things

A CHRISTMAS STORY

THREE MORE CHRISTMAS MONOLOGUES

FOREWORD

You have just put the telephone down following a call in which an apologetic voice tells you that she is so sorry – she can't come to speak to your Branch/Society/Club that evening because she – or a member of her family – has suddenly been taken ill. After murmuring suitable commiserations you hang up the telephone with your mind frantically thinking "what shall we do... a Beetle Drive... a quiz...make a cup of tea and send them all home...?"

This small book may help you in this situation and may provide some enjoyment for your members. Member participation can provide more fun than sitting in rows and listening to a Speaker...so here are a few plays, monologues and stories which might spark off incipient actors, readers, or even Speakers! All the items have been tried and tested in my own church, Sunday School and Mothers' Union Branches.... so have a go... have fun!

IF YOU'VE GOT GOOD NEWS YOU WANT TO SHARE IT

CHARACTERS

Grandma
Mother
Daughter Glenys
Elaine (Mothers' Union Member)
Julie " " "

GRANDMA AND MOTHER TALKING – PRAM IN THE BACKGROUND

MOTHER: So after I'd seen the Rector I went to the King's Arms Hotel.

GRANDMA: Have you consulted Glenys and Tom about all this?

MOTHER: Oh, they'll keep putting it off... someone's got to...

ENTER GLENYS, OBVIOUSLY CROSS

GLENYS: Someone's got to what? What've you been doing, Mum?

MOTHER: Only what's right! I called on the Rector to ask him about Gareth being christened...

GLENYS: Don't you think you should have asked me and Tom first? He's <u>our</u> baby, you know!

MOTHER: He's my grandchild! He's three months old and it's high time he was christened – I had you christened when you were four weeks old...

GRANDMA: Yes, and she was sick all down the Rector's surplice!

MOTHER: Be quiet, Grandma!

GLENYS: We're not sure we want to have Gareth christened, anyway....Tom says, let him grow up and choose for himself.

MOTHER: Tom doesn't know anything about it. His family don't go to church...

GLENYS: Neither do we, most of the time....

MOTHER: Yes, we do – at Christmas and Harvest – and you were married in church....

GLENYS: Yes, and we were asked to make all sorts of promises that we had no intention of keeping...

GRANDMA: Like bringing up children in the Christian faith.

GLENYS: Exactly – so why should we make the sort of promises you have to make at a christening if we're not going to carry them out? It's hypocritical!

MOTHER: I don't know about that – but I do know that babies should be christened – they come on better – and what will people think if he isn't done? It would be so nice – we could have a party at the Kings Arms...

GLENYS: Yes, and that's another thing – if you have a christening you've got to have a party afterwards – everyone expects it – and it costs the earth, especially the drinks!

GRANDMA: It was a cup of tea and a bit of cake in my day...

GLENYS: You know we're saving up to buy a house – that'll be more to Gareth's advantage than a christening and a party he's too young to enjoy... what <u>did</u> you arrange with the Rector, anyway?

MOTHER: He said first of all two Mothers' Union members would come to see you...

GLENYS: What on earth for? I don't want two old girls coming preaching at me!

MOTHER: And then he would want to see you and Tom...

GRANDMA: (LOOKING OUT OF WINDOW) There are two women coming up our path...

MOTHER: That'll be the Mothers' Union members... now, Glenys, do be pleasant...

GLENYS: (GOING TO THE DOOR) I'll soon see them off – like I do with the Jehovah's Witnesses... sorry, we're busy just now...oh – it's Elaine and Julie...I thought it might be.... someone else... do come in..

(ENTER ELAINE AND JULIE)

ELAINE: Are you sure... we can come again... we know what it's like with a young baby... not a minute to spare...

GLENYS: Oh, no – do sit down.... it's lovely to see you... it's been ages ...I used to see you at the Drama group... didn't we have some fun!

JULIE: We did! Remember that time when we did the panto – and everything went wrong! But how are you getting on? May I peep at him? (LOOKS IN PRAM) Oh, he's beautiful! Is he good?

GLENYS: Still awful at night!

MOTHER: I've told her and told her – put him on Cow and Gate – but will she listen...

GRANDMA: Nature's best!

ELAINE: It's hard when you don't get your sleep – makes you feel like a zombie...

GLENYS: I know – life seems to be nothing but feeding and changing nappies and washing...

JULIE: I couldn't believe that one small scrap could make such a lot of washing – but it does pass. When I look back on Daniel's first six months I wonder how I got through... but all of a sudden it seems to get better...

GLENYS: Oh, it is nice to see you! I'm so glad you came – was it for something special?

ELAINE: Yes, we're Mothers' Union members and we visit parents who are thinking of having their babies baptised.

GLENYS: (SHOCKED) You don't mean – that you are in the Mothers' Union – and – go to church!

GRANDMA: That sounds as if you think they go to a house of ill fame!

MOTHER: Be quiet, Grandma!

JULIE: I started going when Daniel was christened – the Rector asked us to come and we thought we'd give it a go – and we were made so welcome and enjoyed the service so much that we're really into it now – I've joined the MU and I teach in Sunday School – it's great, you feel that you're part of a family.

GLENYS: But – I always thought that church was, was – well – boring – and telling you not to do things – what do you really get out of it?

ELAINE: I felt just like you – we had a dreadful time when Jenny was born – you know she was premature – and for a bit we didn't know if she was going to make it... then the Sister in the ward asked me if I'd like Jenny to be baptised. I was a bit sharp with her, asked what difference that would make... she said that God loved Jenny even more than we did – and by having her baptised we were – sort of – holding her in the light of God's love.

GLENYS: (WIPING HER EYES) I'd no idea....

ELAINE: And that helped us, too – and I knew that whatever happened she was safe in God's hands... and I felt quite calm and so did Jack... and – well – you know she got better... and now she is part of the Church family too.

GLENYS: Look, we'll come and see the Rector – I'd like to talk about this some more – we both want the very best for Gareth. I'm glad you came... but tell me – why do you call on people?

JULIE: Well, I suppose – when you've got good news you want to share it... don't you?

THE FAMILY – WHAT ABOUT IT?

Scene: The annual Meals on Wheels helpers' lunch – characters sitting round a table finishing with coffee.

CHARACTERS

Fiona (a 'women's libber')
Sarah (old fashioned)
Jane (young and flippant, married with children)
Carol (a Mothers' Union member)
Glenys " " "
Alice (elderly, cheerful)
Catrin (elderly, single)

JANE: Well, it's nice to be served lunch for a change instead of driving round with Meals on Wheels for our old dears.

SARAH: Not so much of your old dears – I'm older than some of our MOW people – I could have meals but I don't. Some days my arthritis is so bad that I can't get out of bed – but I soldier on –

ALICE: Why don't you apply for Meals on Wheels then?

SARAH: As if I would! I've never been beholden to anybody and I'm not starting now. But if I do get past it I shall expect my family to rally round. I've brought them up to know what's right! There'd be no need for all these social services if families did their duty and looked after their old people themselves.

CATRIN: What if you haven't any family?

FIONA: That's all old hat! Why should women sacrifice themselves and their careers? It's always the women who have to do it – you don't often find men tied to the home looking after Granny.

GLENYS: Life's so different now. Young women have to work, they can't stay at home, even if they would like to – families couldn't manage financially.... mortgages, or high rents... and children's clothes so expensive...

SARAH: They don't need all the things that they've got to have! We were content with a small house – we didn't have washing machines and tellies – we made our children's clothes...

JANE: (SINGS QUIETLY) Tell me the old, old story...

ALICE: I admire young couples nowadays – they're out at work all day, then they come home in the evening and get the meal and do the chores together. And the children are mostly well looked after.

SARAH: I don't agree – what about all those kids on the estate – running wild until well after dark – little vandals, most of them! Their parents don't know where they are and don't care – and then there's all this child abuse – and these murders – it never used to be like this!

CATRIN: Oh, yes, it did – haven't you read Dickens? Or Charles Kingsley? Children had a terrible time of it in the Victorian age – but it didn't get talked about as it does now.

SARAH: Well, respectable people weren't afraid to walk out after dark in this town like they are now! What is this church of yours doing about that, I'd like to know? (GLARES AT CAROL AND GLENYS)

GLENYS: Plenty! We've got a children's club on your estate and a Mother and Toddler group – the Mothers' Union supports Christian family life...

FIONA: The family's on its way out – and a good thing, if you ask me! This idea of the family does more harm than good. Why is it taken for granted that a group of people, just because they are related by blood, be tied together for life? They may not even like each other –

SARAH: Blood's thicker than water!

JANE: A mum has to look after her baby – even a cat stays with her kittens until they are old enough to fend for themselves – and birds build nests... but I must admit, I feel like flying out of our nest sometimes! When the kids are playing up and Jack comes home like a bear with a sore head!

SARAH: There have always been families – parents and children. You can't alter that.

FIONA: Why can't you? Like Jane said, once the birds have flown from the nest there's no need for the mother to stay there – better for the kids, too. My parents smothered me – wouldn't let me take a job away from home, always asking me questions. Even after I was married they were always around, interfering – it's smother love, not mother love.

CAROL: But a family needn't be like that – the family situation should be where the members are able to grow and develop.

JANE: And then fly away – take off – more like a launching pad! So long as they come home sometimes.

FIONA: Well, you haven't convinced me! Why have there got to be these tight little groups? Just because it's always been like that?

CATRIN: Actually, it hasn't always been like that. In ancient Roman society what was meant by 'the family' was the whole household – not only blood relations but the servants and slaves as well. 'Family' can mean a group of people.

JANE: Like a commune or a kibbutz – I think that might be fun – all share in looking after the children. I'd go for that!

SARAH: That's like these hippies – or New Age travellers – sharing husbands – disgraceful!

FIONA: Anyone can share mine!

GLENYS: You don't mean that –

FIONA: I'm not well up on the Bible – but I do remember that Jesus said you've got to hate your family.

ALICE: I'm sure he didn't!

CAROL: Well – yes, he did. He said "If anyone comes to me and does not hate his own father and mother and wife and children and brothers and sisters, yes, and even his own life, he cannot be my disciple". And he also said, when his family came to take him home, thinking that he was mad, "Who are my mother and my brothers? Whoever does the will of God is my family".

CATRIN: I must admit that's always worried me.

FIONA: So what do you make of that, you MU members? Jesus didn't think much of family life, did he?

CAROL: Oh, yes he did! He often called God his father – sometimes he called him 'Abba' which means 'Dad' – and this familiarity with God was something quite new for Jews. And when his disciples asked him to teach them to pray he said "Start by saying 'Our Father'.... " and St. Paul talks about God as 'the Father, from whom every family in heaven and on earth is named'. So it looks as if family life starts with God.

GLENYS: And when Jesus was dying on the Cross he asked his friend John to look after his Mother – just think, even when he was in such agony he thought about Mary.

CAROL: I think when he talked about hating relatives and that those who did God's will being his family, he was using extreme language to emphasise that a Christian's first loyalty should be to God – and that should come even before family ties.

CATRIN: I suppose that's what we mean by the Church being a family – it's a great comfort to me because I haven't any blood relations - except cousins in Australia – but I do feel I've got a family in the Church.

CAROL: Of course you have, love – if people don't feel loved and accepted as they are, then we've no right to call ourselves a church at all!

SARAH: But we've got to keep up our standards – I'm very worried about that family that have started coming to church - they come in late, the children make a terrible noise – and now they want to have the three youngest baptised.

ALICE: The Scattergoods, do you mean? I'm glad to see them – what does a bit of noise matter?

SARAH: The noise isn't the worst – I know for a fact that the parents aren't married! They've been living together for years!

JANE: They've done well to stick together then, living in that dreadful house with all those kids and Jim Scattergood out of work. They must be committed to each other and the kids to stay together. I'd have walked out of that mess years ago.

SARAH: Committed? Irresponsible, I should say! They're a drain on the Social Services. And – you might not know this – but – (IMPRESSIVE PAUSE)

CATRIN: I expect we shall soon, because you're going to tell us!

SARAH: Well – it ought to be known! One of the babies being christened is the Scattergood's eldest daughter's child.

ALICE: We do know about Donna's baby – poor girl, she's only fourteen. It happens nowadays - it's not for us to sit in judgement.

SARAH: But they'll just go on having babies regardless – living that way is wrong – surely the Church should keep up standards?

CAROL: What did Jesus say about the woman taken in adultery?

(DEAD SILENCE)

JANE: Neither do I condemn thee.

SARAH: But didn't he then say "Go and sin no more"?

GLENYS: And what is the best way to help a family carry out that command?

CAROL: By accepting them and meeting them with love – it's only when children feel secure in a loving relationship that you can begin to show them how to follow Christ.

GLENYS: If they can be brought into the family of the Church then we can leave it to God – Marlene Scattergood was talking to me when I took their Grandma's dinner last week. She said that since they had started coming to church she and Jim were thinking of tying the knot – they'd just never got round to it before!

JANE: Been too busy, I expect.... bless them....

CAROL: I've got an idea – something that the Mothers' Union could do to help our church do even more to become a caring family. Could members – not just MU members but church members too – adopt a family? We'd get the opportunity when a baby is baptised – or a couple get married – or when someone is ill....

FIONA: They might not want you...

GLENYS: How do we know until we try it? I think it's a great idea! It'd have to be tactfully done – but no one minds a friendly smile and someone calling to say "How are you?" It could be built up from there...

ALICE: Who's for more coffee? We're going to need strength if we're going to do all this!

CAROL: We can get strength all right – remember what Paul said?

SARAH: Paul?

CATRIN: Paul of Tarsus – he said "I can do all things through Christ who strengthens me".

ALICE: We'll be all right then! Coffee?

SUPPER AT MARTHA'S

CHARACTERS

Jesus
Martha
Mary
Laz

NARRATOR: The scene is Martha's house in Bethany. She lives with her younger sister, Mary, a philosophy student (INDICATES MARY, SITTING RIGHT, READING) and her young brother, Lazarus, a sixth form schoolboy MARTHA IS BUSTLING ABOUT, FLAPPING A DUSTER.

MARTHA: This place is a mess.... (CALLS) Mary! Take your head out of that book and come and tidy up....

MARY: In a minute....

(ENTER LAZ)

LAZ: Hey, girls! We're going to have a visitor for supper - I met him in the School Canteen – he's a nice chap – no side to him....

MARY: What's his name?

LAZ: Jesus.

MARY: Oh, that's wonderful! I met him yesterday in the Union.....

MARTHA: (INTERRUPTS) It isn't wonderful at all! - I've only got soup for supper – oh, dear, I'll have to make one of my cheese omelettes.

MARY: Oh, don't bother ....he won't mind....

LAZ: Here he is!

(ENTER JESUS, MARTHA RUSHES OFF LEFT)

LAZ: Come in and sit down –
Here is Mary ..... Martha (LOOKS ROUND)
Oh – she's gone to the kitchen....

JESUS: It's good to be with you. (SITS, MARY SITS ON THE FLOOR)

MARY: Jesus – when I saw you at the meeting yesterday you were talking about your Father's Kingdom.... Where is it – is it far? Can we go there?

JESUS: It's nearer than you think – yes – you can be there...

(THERE IS A CLASH OF SAUCEPANS OFF STAGE AND MARTHA ENTERS, VERY CROSS)

MARTHA: Mary! Come and give me a hand! Lay the table – I can't do everything...Jesus, tell her to help me!

JESUS: (GENTLY) Dear Martha – you are so busy – but Mary is right to talk with me – and I would like you to sit down and listen, too…. Send Laz out for fish and chips…

LAZ: Wicked! I like fish and chips! I've got the money (RUSHES OUT)

MARTHA: But –

JESUS: Relax, Martha dear - we'll eat round the fire and enjoy each other's company.

MARY: Come and sit down, love, come and listen to Jesus – I'm sorry I left you to do it all..... I'll make the tea.

EXITS AND RETURNS WITH TRAY WITH TEAPOT AND MUGS. ENTER LAZ WITH NEWSPAPER PARCEL OF FISH AND CHIPS, DISTRIBUTES THEM WITH LAUGHTER

JESUS: Thank you. Father, for all your gifts....

ALL: Amen

ANYONE FOR TENNIS?

CHARACTERS

Mildred (a lady of the old school)
Rhiannon (young, light-hearted)
Nerys (keen on money-making and organising)
Evelyn (a rather helpless, fluttery lady)
Gwen (the leader)

SCENE - The monthly Mothers' Union meeting at St. Cawdraf's

GWEN: Now, we haven't got a Speaker for this evening because we really must discuss our programme for the coming year and decide what we're going to do....

NERYS: Have you booked somewhere for the Outing yet?

GWEN: I'll come to that later – the theme for this year is Relationships –and of course this theme is utterly reliant on our theme of a few years ago - Love and Service.

RHIANNON: Sounds like tennis – how about it, girls?

MILDRED: We're not talking about games –

RHIANNON: It would be fun if we were...

GWEN: Let's get on, shall we – now, let's think what we can do in the community to love and serve people.

RHIANNON: How about a tennis tournament between us and the clerics? It would be an entertainment for people to see us – and the clerics – in shorts!

MILDRED: No one is going to see me in shorts!

NERYS: A nice coffee morning with a raffle – we could make quite a lot of money –

EVELYN: Oh, do let's get away from coffee mornings and making money – it's so sordid – what about something really uplifting – like a quiet day of prayer in church?

MILDRED: That's not going to appeal to the folk on this estate – most only come to church for christenings and funerals.

GWEN: Thank you, Evelyn, for reminding us about prayer – of course, that's the mainspring of all our work – but Mildred's right, too – I think we have to get alongside people, get to know them before we can begin to talk about our faith and prayer.

RHIANNON: That's right – my next door neighbours wouldn't come near a church – they think I'm mad – got religious mania or something – but they're a lovely family – the kids play with ours and they get on fine – I did ask if they'd like to come to Sunday School with ours – but they all go out walking on a Sunday –

GWEN: Well, it's good that families go out and enjoy the countryside together – I've often thought we should change the times that we hold Sunday School and church services to fit in with present-day family life – the

Wednesday Club at St. Cyprian's is a sort of week day Sunday School.

MILDRED: I don't approve of that at all! Sunday is the Lord's day. When I was young we –

RHIANNON: Yes, I know, you went to church and Sunday School three times on a Sunday...I think a weekday Sunday School is a very good idea – we'd get more children there – if they had it after school the mums would be glad to get their little darlings out of the way whilst they made the evening meal – we could give the children orange squash and biscuits, and have some playing and then Christian teaching... I'd help with it.

NERYS: You'd have to charge! People don't value things they get free -

MILDRED: Why should we take the kids just to give the mothers time to cook?... If they didn't go out to work...

GWEN: (FIRMLY) Because what we're trying to do is loving and serving....that is how we can establish relationships with our neighbours.

EVELYN: (PLAINTIVELY) It would be very hard to love and serve my neighbours – the noise they make is terrible – they can't seem to control their children at all – the father shouts and the mother cries....

RHIANNON: Have you tried talking to them – making friends with them?

EVELYN: Well – no .... but she did say to me that she wished she could get some advice about bringing up her children.

GWEN: There's your opportunity! The MU will form a Parenting group – some of our members have been on a parenting training course.... it was a great help to me when my children were young.

MILDRED: (SNIFFS) Parenting! We never needed anything like that when my children were young. Discipline! That's what's lacking nowadays. I made my children go to Sunday School – they had to do what they were told, mind their manners and eat what was put in front of them – and have a dose of Syrup of Figs every Friday night – I never had any trouble with them!

RHIANNON: (WINKS AT THE OTHERS) What did they think about Sunday School and Syrup of Figs?

MILDRED: Never asked them! There's too much half-baked psychology nowadays.

EVELYN: There are a lot of unhappy families nowadays, too – whatever the cause. I will talk to Joan next door – I feel sorry for her – she was married very young – she's not much more than a child herself....

RHIANNON: And I'll have a word with my neighbours – I'm sure their children would come to a Wednesday Club – something in the week...

NERYS: What's this Contact Centre all about? I heard two women talking about it on the bus.

GWEN: Oh, yes – the Mothers' Union help with that – it's a place where divorced parents can meet their children for a couple of hours.

RHIANNON: What if the parents meet? There could be stand-up fighting!

GWEN: No – that's carefully monitored - there are separate rooms. There is so much sadness when a parent can't see his – or her - children. Helping at the Contact Centre really is carrying out our Fifth Object...to help families in adversity.

MILDRED: (TO EVERYONES ASTONISHMENT) I wouldn't mind helping with that. There's a lot of divorce about nowadays.

RHIANNON: Sounds like flu....

MILDRED: I told my husband when we were first married that I wouldn't stand any hanky-panky!

RHIANNON: Did you give him Syrup of Figs too?

GWEN: Hush, Rhiannon – thank you, Mildred, I'll put your name down for the training.

MILDRED: Training? At my age! Oh, well, I'll go along with it. I suppose this is what loving and serving is all about –

RHIANNON: I still think we should have a tennis match with the clerics - I believe that new curate at St. Cyprian's is very athletic ...

NERYS: (SUDDENLY INSPIRED) How about a fun day in and around the Community Centre? We could have games outside – and refreshments – and a bouncy castle for the children – a quiet corner if people wanted to be quiet or to talk to someone about problems – we wouldn't charge...

RHIANNON: I can't believe I'm hearing this! Are you feeling all right, Nerys?

NERYS: Yes – I'm remembering the sermon last Sunday – about Jesus going to people where they are – most people go to the Community Centre for one thing or another.

GWEN: Thank you Nerys – that's a great idea and we'll get on with it – it really <u>is</u> about loving and serving our community.

NERYS: We still haven't talked about the Outing. Where are we going?

GWEN: (SEEING THAT NERYS IS DETERMINED TO GET THIS SETTLED) All right – where would you all like to go?

MEMBERS: (ALL TOGETHER) Chester...Llangollen.... go on the canal...

EVELYN: The coach fare is so dear nowadays –

GWEN: What about Llandudno ? (OR ANY OTHER TOWN IN YOUR LOCALITY) It's not too far.... lovely shops – the seaside – all sorts of activities for children.

EVELYN: Yes, but we don't have children on our Outing.

RHIANNON: Well, perhaps it's time we did! If we get a Parenting group going and a Wednesday Club running, then we could ask parents and children to come with us – fill the coach – have two coaches....

MILDRED: You're getting carried away! Do you really think they'd come?

RHIANNON: Yes – if we make friends with them first – relationships – loving and serving – that's what it's all about! Isn't it?

WHY ARE WE DOING THIS PRAYER GROUP THING?

CHARACTERS

Bethan (young, enthusiastic)
Mair (the leader)
Priscilla (elderly, set in her ways)
Angharad (outspoken)
Meriel (soothing)

ANGHARAD: Well, I've come, but I don't see the point of it really – if we want to go to a prayer group we can go to the Vicar's Bible Study meeting – we don't need this, as well.

PRISCILLA: But you never go to the Vicar's Bible study....

ANGHARAD: No, but I could if wanted to, couldn't I? I don't go because it's Bingo on a Wednesday evening.

BETHAN: It's Yoga on a Wednesday evening, too.

PRISCILLA: Surely you don't go to Yoga – lying on the floor!

BETHAN: It is a bit cold – but I put Jack's longjohns on under my leotards – it's really good – and we keep saying a cointreau –

ANGHARAD: A what?

BETHAN: A cointreau – over and over again – it makes the exercises meaningful.

MERIEL: She means a mantra.

BETHAN: That's right, a cointreau – oh, I do enjoy it, and the instructor's lovely – next week he's going to show us how to put one leg behind our heads!

PRISCILLA: Sounds dangerous – tying yourself in knots – you be careful! But I'd like to know just why we're doing this prayer group thing instead of our usual meeting with a Speaker.

MAIR: I explained that at the last meeting – the Faith and Policy Unit have got these lovely ideas for prayer groups...and our Third Object is to maintain a world-wide fellowship of Christians united in prayer, worship and service. Prayer should be the mainspring of everything else that we do...

PRISCILLA: What more can we do, I'd like to know? I think our job is to help the Vicar by doing the teas and cleaning the church and so on – I'm too old for prayer meetings and study groups.

ANGHARAD: Yes, and we should be doing something about the brasses in church – they're a disgrace – no one's cleaned them for weeks!

BETHAN: I heard of a good way to clean brasses – it was at my Green folklore meeting – you put them all in a bucket and boil them up with some rhubarb leaves –

ANGHARAD: And do you say a cointreau over them?

MERIEL: Sshh – do let Mair tell us more about having a prayer group.

MAIR: It's very simple – we take a short passage from the Gospels and someone reads it – then we have twenty minutes of silence to read it over ourselves and reflect on it...what it means to us.... perhaps we ask the Lord to speak to us....and then the passage is read aloud again and we are invited – but only if we wish - to share our thoughts with each other.... it can be a lovely, peaceful time together.

PRISCILLA: Sounds a bit mystical to me... not my sort of thing at all! Anyway, we <u>do</u> pray together in our Branch meetings – and we all go to church – when we can – and we pray then, surely?

MAIR: Yes, of course we do... but I think these prayer meetings helps us to look at prayer – to experience more deeply prayer as a relationship with God.

BETHAN I say my prayers in the bath.

ANGHARAD: <u>What</u>?

BETHAN: In the bath. It's the only place I can be on my own with the kids around all the time. It's nice and warm and peaceful.

PRISCILLA: (DEEPLY SHOCKED) But – in the bath! With no clothes on! That's no way to come before the Almighty! Before I go to bed I have a good wash and brush my hair and put on my nightie – <u>and</u> my dressing gown – and compose my mind – then I kneel by my bed and say my prayers.

ANGHARAD: Will you be wearing your dressing gown when you go to Heaven, do you think?

MERIEL: Sshh – I think we should pray wherever we feel most comfortable. I mostly pray sitting at the kitchen table when everyone's gone out. I'd be too tired to pray at night like you do, Priscilla – I'd go to sleep with my face in the duvet.

ANGHARAD: I say my prayers in bed – Fred would think I'd gone mad if I knelt by the bed – he'd be most uncomfortable.

BETHAN: Why are we so self conscious about praying? It's like talking to a friend.

PRISCILLA: Because it's a very private thing – I'd hate to pray out loud like they do in some churches – it's between me and God. It's nothing to do with other people.

ANGHARAD: You'd say you'd got your spiritual life all sorted out, would you?

MAIR: (DISMAYED) Angharad – don't –

ANGHARAD: I'm not being nasty – I really want to know – because I haven't –got this sort of thing sorted out, I mean. There's Bethan saying that talking to God is like being with a friend – I don't feel like that at all – God seems far away – it's like tossing messages into outer space – it's like knocking on a door and not getting an answer....

MERIEL: God isn't far away.... he's with us – 'closer than breathing, closer than hands and feet'. Jesus promised his friends – and that's you and me – that he would be with them always – his Spirit would come.... do you remember that hymn 'Lord of the Dance? In the last verse it quotes the words of Jesus –"I am the life that will never, never die

– and I'll live in you if you'll live in me"....Jesus isn't far away – and Bethan's right – it is like talking - and listening - to a friend.

ANGHARAD: (SLOWLY) If that's really true – it would be marvellous.....all right – let's give it a go....

MAIR: Right – let's get started..... I've got print outs of the Stilling of the Storm.....

NO ROOM AT THE INN?

CHARACTERS

GWYNETH (Mayoress)
ISABEL (Her sister)
ELIN (Gwyneth's daughter, between ten and sixteen)
MARION (Gwyneth's elder daughter)

GWYNETH AND ISABEL ARE SITTING DRINKING TEA, ELIN READING.

GWYNETH: I'm glad you came round – it's made me sit down - I'm absolutely worn out!

ISABEL: Good heavens, why? What's happened?

GWYNETH: Everything! Christmas! I've just about had enough of it – and it's not here yet.

ISABEL: Whatever's wrong now?

GWYNETH: There's so much to do – ever since George was made mayor –

ISABEL: You were keen enough to be mayoress!

GWYNETH: But there's so much going on - there's the Civic Reception tomorrow evening – and the children's party the day after... and I haven't finished my Christmas shopping... I wish Christmas was over... I can't think why we have it!

ELIN: We have it because of Jesus being born!

SILENCE

GWYNETH: Well – I know that – but that's got nothing to do with all the rushing around that I have to do.

ELIN: Why do you do it, then?

GWYNETH: Don't be cheeky, Elin – I've got to go to all these functions to support your Dad and as well as that buy everyone presents and cook a huge Christmas dinner.

ELIN: But that's not about Jesus – nobody wanted him – he had to be born in a stable – I don't suppose Mary and Joseph had a turkey dinner – we ought to think about him – are we going to church on Christmas Day?

GWYNETH: Church on Christmas morning! With all the dinner to cook?

ISABEL: It's nice to go to Church at Christmas if you've got the time – I certainly haven't – but tell me- is your Marion coming home for Christmas?

GWYNETH: Oh, no – the baby's due soon – I've told them not to come…

ELIN: I wish she would come – then the baby might be born here – at Christmas! Christmas – wouldn't that be cool?

GWYNETH: No, it wouldn't! I've too much on my plate at the moment to cope with a baby.

ISABEL: Is she going back to college later? You've not really forgiven her for starting a family so young, have you?

GWYNETH: Well I have to say we're very disappointed – she had a brilliant career in front of her…. I can't think what she'll do now…

ELIN: She'll have a baby to love….isn't that more important than an old career….I think it's mean that you don't want her to come home – it's just like Mary and Baby Jesus – nobody wanted them!

GWYNETH: Elin, be quiet! You're getting far too uppity since you went to that Youth Club – religion is all very well – but not at Christmas when everyone's so busy…..

ISABEL: There's someone at the door….

ENTER MARION, CARRYING BABY

MARION: Hi, Mum – we thought we would surprise you - meet James - your first grandchild.

GWYNETH:
ISABEL: (together) What?......When...?

MARION; He was born two days ago....

ISABEL: Where is David?

MARION: Putting the car away – well, Mum, is there going to be room at the inn for us?

ELIN: (RUSHES TO HUG MARION) Of course there is - you can have my bed – oh look at him... isn't he beautiful?

MARION: Well, Mum? (SHE GOES RIGHT UP TO GWYNETH AND SHOWS HER THE BABY... GWYNETH SLOWLY TAKES THE BABY IN HER ARMS)

GWYNETH: (TEARFULLY) Oh, Marion – I'm sorry for the way I've behaved to you – and your baby – I see now – he's lovely – he's a new life ... and that makes everything different...

ELIN: It's just like Jesus coming – he made everything different! Can James come to church with me on Christmas morning?

CHRISTMAS EVE IN THE KING'S ARMS KITCHEN

CHARACTERS

Sara
Gwen
Rhiannon

GWEN: My feet are killing me – what time do you think we'll finish tonight?

SARA: I'm going at eleven, whether we've finished or not – surely they won't be wanting food after that.

RHIANNON: I want to go to church – the Midnight service starts at half past eleven.

GWEN: Church? Whatever for?

RHIANNON: Well….. it's Christmas…….

SARA: That's all very well, very nice I suppose if you've got time…..but I've far too much to do to go to church at Christmas…… I've got all Dan's family coming tomorrow…. I'm sick of the sight of turkey ….. I've seen enough turkey dinners here tonight …..

SHOUT FROM OUTSIDE

RHIANNON: All right, I'll go…. (EXIT)

GWEN: That girl's going potty….. fancy wanting to go to church after working all afternoon and evening.

SARA: Don't you knock church….. I sometimes wish I'd got something like that to turn to….life's hard, what with Dan out of work and so grumpy...and the kids wanting all these expensive toys that the others seem to have...

ENTER RHIANNON

RHIANNON: Two turkey dinners and one lasagne…..and a couple have just come in, asked for a bed….

SARA GETS PLATES

GWEN: We're full…..they must be mad, expecting a bed at this time of night…..

RHIANNON: I felt sorry for them….. she's pregnant…..

GWEN: Well, I'm not sorry for them…. They should have more sense…. Who are they, anyway – where have they come from?

RHIANNON: The man said they had come a long way…. But they had to come…. I don't know why.

(TAKES PLATES FROM SARA, EXITS)

SARA: I wonder if they're some sort of refugees…. or those travellers……

GWEN: We don't want them here if they are….. I've no patience with it…..refugees….the health service is overloaded as it is... I've got to wait twelve months to have my bunions done. The clinic was full of Indians.... and as for travellers - gypsies – they probably don't pay any rates... it's not fair on respectable people!

ENTER RHIANNON

SARA: What happened to those people…. The refugees…..?

RHIANNON: That poor girl looked in pain…. The man said "Haven't you got anywhere we can go?" And then Reuben said very reluctantly "All right, you can kip down in the shed" .... and the girl said to her man "Don't worry Joe, I'll be all right – God is looking after us".

SARA: But – in the shed, I'm going to get a duvet and a pillow from the linen room….

GWEN: You'll catch it if Reuben finds out!

SARA: Don't care – I'm sorry for them – (EXITS)

RHIANNON: That girl – she's so calm – I can't understand it…. And she's got a lovely face.

GWEN: Lovely face!… that's all very well, but what was her family thinking of, letting her wander about in her condition? She should be at home.

RHIANNON: Perhaps they haven't got a home.

(ENTER SARA)

SARA: That poor girl is in labour – I'm going to phone for an ambulance.

RHIANNON: The ambulance men are on strike –

SARA: Whatever are we going to do? Gwen – you used to be a midwife…. You'd better go and see them.

GWEN: Oh, all right…. And you two had better get on with the washing up. (EXIT)

SARA: I'm all to pieces…..she was in such pain….. and her husband was so worried…

RHIANNON: She's got Gwen now….for all her hard words, Gwen's as soft as butter really.

SARA: Yes…. I suppose we'd better get on with that washing up….. THEY GO TO SIDE AND MOVE A FEW DISHES

RHIANNON: Listen!

SARAH: What?

RHIANNON Listen!

(A BABY'S CRY)

SARA: Oh! The baby's here!

RHIANNON: And – you know what night it is?

SARA: It's Christmas Eve – why….

RHIANNON: It's just a traveller's baby – yet Jesus said "Whoever welcomes one of these little ones welcomes me".

SARA: I don't know about that....

ENTER GWEN – SHE IS HOLDING BACK TEARS

GWEN: Oh, girls - the baby's here - I delivered him - he's beautiful - I must get some warm water –Sara, heat up some soup for them.....

SARA: We'll be in trouble with Reuben....

GWEN: I don't care – this is more important....it's new life..... and - oh, I'm an old fool – but it's love as well.... I shall go to church tomorrow..... it's what Christmas is all about....come on, Sara, have you got that soup....let's all go and see them....

NARRATOR: "....and they said....Let us go to Bethlehem and see this thing that has happened which the Lord has made known to us". (Luke 2.15)

CHRISTMAS WITH MARY

CHARACTERS

Bethan
Glenys

BETHAN: Come on, sit down and have a cup of tea - you look fed up!

GLENYS: I am fed up – Christmas is getting me down… I've just been shopping or trying to shop... Tesco's is like a mad house – and all the shops I went in had Christmas carols blaring out so that you couldn't hear yourself think.

BETHAN: It's awful, I know – and it seems to get worse everywhere – it takes away from the real meaning of Christmas

GLENYS: What is the real meaning of Christmas anyway? I'm beginning to think that all it means is buying presents I can't afford (Gareth wants a lap-top!) And food and drink so that everyone can eat and drink themselves silly.... how did it get like this?

BETHAN: I suppose it's the shops trying to make more money … all that advertising.. .. and it all seems to fall on the women… shopping and cooking and keeping everyone happy… we've got Tom's sister and her husband

and my old Uncle Cadwaladr coming for Christmas… he's bound to say something to upset the in-laws… they're so prim and proper and Cadwaladr will tell one of his jokes…. When they arrived last year he told Agnes that he'd mistaken her for the turkey! She wasn't amused! When things get really hectic I try to think about Mary….

GLENYS: Mary?

BETHAN: Yes – we did a play in Mothers' Union about walking with Mary.

GLENYS: I don't feel I could walk with Mary…. It's all so long ago…. And she seems far away – she was a saint – not like us.

BETHAN: Perhaps saints are ordinary people… like us.

GLENYS: But think of Mary's life – an angel coming to her – and being told she was to be mother of the Son of God – that's not ordinary at all - she was set apart, someone really special – I don't think we can get anywhere near her.

BETHAN: You're right, of course – that Mary was unique. But she was a woman like we are – and she had a baby – like you and me – and she was a working man's wife – an ordinary housewife – we share all that with Mary – and perhaps we can share some of the marvellous things that happened to her.

GLENYS: (DOUBTFULLY) I don't see how – when you see those statues and pictures of Mary with her baby she always looks so calm, so peaceful and smiling - I'm not like that – I can get really cross with my family sometimes – I fly off the handle and yell at them –

BETHAN: I think the artists portray Mary looking saintly because that's how they would like to think of her – but she was a human being – a young girl when the angel came to tell her she was going to have a baby... she must have been terrified – she wasn't yet married... what were people going to say about her? She could have been stoned to death for immorality... we know she was frightened because the angel told her not to be afraid.

GLENYS: I'd have been terrified… I couldn't have faced it….

BETHAN: And then all she went through afterwards – that long journey to Bethlehem, and when she got there her pains were starting – we both know what that's like…. She must have cried for her mother, for someone to help her… the Gospels don't say anything about that – well, Matthew and Luke were men – they don't know what we go through to give birth!

GLENYS: No – poor girl – it must have been awful for her!

BETHAN: I think what helped her was what the angel had said – something about God's Holy Spirit coming, and the power of God – perhaps that's what made her strong.

GLENYS: I could do with that sort of help sometimes – having teenage kids is awful – I worry myself sick if they're late home... but Mary didn't have to put up with that kind of thing. Jesus must have been a model child – you know what the carol says "mild, obedient, good was he" not like my two little horrors!

BETHAN: I'm not so sure about that – what about that time when Jesus went missing when the family went to Jerusalem. Three days he was missing! Mary and Joseph must have been frantic .... and when they did find him Mary was cross "Why have you treated us like this – we've been so worried" she asked him.

GLENYS: I'd have been the same – I clouted our Gareth when he gave us the slip at the fairground last week… what did Jesus think he was doing?

BETHAN: That was just it! He didn't seem to have any idea that he was to blame and he seemed genuinely surprised that they were worried. "Didn't you know that I'd be in my Father's house" he said.

GLENYS: My Father's house? What did he mean? Do you think that's when Jesus realised who he really was – and what his life was going to be?

BETHAN: Yes – and Mary had to accept that he was growing up, away from them – that he had to begin his own life, and that she had to let him go … like I had to when our Peter went on VSO in Africa.

GLENYS: It's not easy, being a parent!

BETHAN: It must have been worse for Mary when Jesus started preaching and healing – she would have heard that the Jewish scribes and priests didn't like what he was doing – his brothers thought he was over the top - so they took Mary with them, to try and make him come home.

GLENYS: And what did Jesus say to that?

BETHAN: When they got to the house, the people there told Jesus that his family were outside, looking for him… but Jesus said "Who are my brothers? Who is my mother?"

GLENYS: That must have hurt Mary! What did he mean?

BETHAN: He looked at the people listening to him and said "Here is my mother – here are my brothers – anyone who obeys God – they are my family"…. he knew that he loved the whole world.

GLENYS: It must have been hard for Mary to take that on board!

BETHAN: There was worse to come. The Jewish authorities and the Romans got rid of Jesus in the end.. and Mary watched him die on the Cross. The old man, Simeon had said that a sword would pierce her heart… but she knew that Jesus loved her – because he told John to look after her, and that John would be her son… and then after three days, she knew that Jesus was alive - how joyful she must have been….

GLENYS: Yes, but I can't imagine how any ordinary woman could have got through all that trauma without having a breakdown.

BETHAN: When the Angel came to Mary he told her that God's Holy Spirit would come to her and that she would be the mother of the Son of God. When you first know you're pregnant you can hardly believe it - that a tiny bunch of cells is going to be a living child growing in you – and for Mary – that was God himself...and then that gave her strength.... and we can get that strength, too.

GLENYS: (SHOCKED) How can it possibly be like that for us?

BETHAN: You know what we say in that prayer in the Communion Service? "That we may evermore live in him and he in us". Jesus told his friends that he would never leave them – that God's Holy Spirit would come to live in them. It's new life - God's life – in us. Like Mary's baby grew in her. That's how we can walk with Mary... That's the real meaning of Christmas, isn't it ? Jesus with us – always.

GLENYS: Yes – you know – I feel quite different.

BETHAN: So do I – I feel able to face it all now…I'll even be nice to old Uncle Cadwalader.....

THREE CHRISTMAS MONOLOGUES

THE NIGHT THAT CHANGED THINGS

The Shepherd's wife's story

Do you ever wonder if your husband's going doolally? Well, I certainly did when Jacob came in this morning! You see, he's a shepherd and they do get a bit strange, being up there with the sheep all the time. But really, this morning – well – I thought he'd gone mad! He said that about midnight there was a sort of light in the sky – and then – someone – he said it was an angel – came and said "Don't be afraid – I've brought you good news – for everyone". Well you can imagine what I said to him "Have you been drinking?" He said, no – and neither had the others – and they ALL saw this – whatever it was, too – and that wasn't all. This – angel – if that's what it was – said "In Bethlehem your Saviour has been born – today – he's the Christ, the Messiah". And then there were a whole lot more angels, filling the sky and singing...

And then – you'll never believe this – they actually left the sheep – and went down to Bethlehem to see – and yes, they did find a baby, just been born – in the stable of the Maccabees inn of all places....

But what I don't understand is the way my Jacob has changed – you know what he's like, very quiet, a bit morose and grumpy sometimes... never says much... but now – well, he's singing and laughing all over the house – actually hugged me! I'm wondering what in heaven's name has happened to him... perhaps I'll go down to the stable – take a lamb's fleece to keep the baby warm.... because that baby's changed things, somehow....

The Innkeeper's wife's story

Who'd do this job? Take last night, it was horrific! Whoever in the government thought up this census wants his head feeling! Everyone to go to the place where his family came from – I ask you! Seems like everyone has their family roots in Bethlehem, judging by the crowds that flocked in last night. All rushing about trying to find accommodation. We were fully booked – had to keep turning people away... but there was one young couple – they worried me. She was heavily pregnant – she looked about fifteen years old – really, these days they've no morals! I blame the parents .The man looked worried sick. My husband was a bit short with them – 'No use coming here, we're full" he said... and then he turned to me – "Shut the door and come in, people want serving".

But – I couldn't shut the door somehow – because the girl suddenly gasped and clutched her back – and I thought she could be starting in labour. I whispered to the man "Go to the stable – it's round the back"... and then I thought 'What a place to have a confinement in'... I took a lamp off the shelf and ran after them with it – they'd need to see, wouldn't they?

And after that – do you know – everything seemed changed somehow – oh, the pub was still full of noisy people, come getting drunk, some just tired out... but I was GLAD to serve them, make them comfortable – and I felt different – sort of – calmer, happier – I don't know why –

except that it's all to do with that girl and her baby. They seemed to have changed thing.

The midwife's story

It's miserable, feeling old and useless! I'm the inn-keeper's mother, and after my husband's death I used to help in the bar – but now, I'm too slow, I can't remember the orders – and my rheumaticks are so bad that I drop things – so I just stay upstairs, out of the way.

But last night was different. I was thinking about going to bed, then I looked out of the window and saw this young couple going into the stable – and I knew I was needed. You see, I was the village midwife until I got too old and they sent that jumped up young miss from Jerusalem with her modern ways... telling the mums to do breathing exercises, would you believe! Raspberry leaf tea and tender loving care is all that needed to bring a babe into the world. Well, I could tell just from looking at that poor lass, that her time had come and that she had no one to help her but a useless man... I got up, put my apron on and went down ... and on the way I got a jug of hot water from the kitchen... no one bothered me, they were all rushing around like headless chickens...

I carried the water to the stable without spilling a drop.... me, who had needed a stick to hobble with for years... but I walked quite easily... and when I got there... well – I was just in time! All my old skills came back – it was lovely to be working again – I delivered a beautiful baby boy and put him in his mum's arms...and she was radiant! I tidied them up, then I went and pinched some wine and bread from the kitchen for them... they needed it after all they'd gone through... and then I left them and went to bed.

And this morning I felt wonderful! I'm still stiff and aching – but I don't mind any more – and I don't feel cross and frustrated like I did before. Last night I felt there was nothing to look forward to... now I feel full of hope. Something's changed.....

A CHRISTMAS STORY

AN UNEXPECTED ANGEL

The Crib service was over and the Vicar was showing the Sunday School children the Crib set up ready for the Christmas services later that week. The children gazed fascinated at the Holy Family, the shepherds and the animals

"Is that cow going to eat Baby Jesus?" enquired Billy, a lively six-year-old.

"No, of course not" said the Vicar, moving the cow which indeed seemed to hovering over the manger.

Old Jacob, the verger, was switching lights off and muttering. He was cranky at the best of times and Christmas, with all the extra services, the Crib, the Christmas tree and the lights to put up, had tried his patience to the uttermost. "Kids!" he muttered, picking up toffee papers from the floor with a groan.

"Right, let's find your Mums and Dads in the Church Hall", said the Vicar and they all went out. All except four-year-old Daisy. She lingered by the Crib, looking lovingly at the Baby in the manger. She thought he looked lonely by himself in there and wished that Mary could pick him up and cuddle him. She would love to cuddle him. Greatly daring she picked the baby up and hugged him, kissing his head. "I love you, Jesus" she whispered.

A sudden noise behind her made her jump and to her horror she saw the verger looming up. She tried to put the little figure back in the manger but in her fright she dropped him on the floor and his head came off! Appalled, she gazed at this tragedy and burst into tears.

"Now see what you've done!" growled Jacob. "That's what comes of touching things you shouldn't! Go on, get off home"

"I only wanted to cuddle him" sobbed Daisy, and crept out.

Her family were just about to leave when she joined them. "Come on, Daisy, where have you been, it's time we went home" her mother said, not noticing her woebegone face. When they got home it was bedtime and she was too ashamed to tell anyone what had happened. But when she was in bed, in the dark she said her prayers and added a fervent petition. "Please, God, send an angel to mend Baby Jesus!"

Daisy's mother couldn't understand why her daughter seemed reluctant to go to church on Christmas morning. "I've got a cold", muttered Daisy.

"No you haven't – come along and don't be silly".

During the service the Vicar summoned all the children to come and gather round the Crib. Daisy felt sick. Now her crime was going to be discovered. "Come on, Daisy, you can't see there, come to the front", said the Vicar kindly, wondering why the child looked so terrified. Fearfully, Daisy crept to the font and looked at the crib, at

Mary and Joseph and at Baby Jesus – he was all right! A broad smile spread over Daisy's face.

"An angel did come" she shouted.

No one knew what she meant. But the old verger felt an unusual warmth round his heart. He fingered the tube of glue in his pocket. "Never been taken for an angel before", he muttered.

THREE MORE CHRISTMAS MONOLOGUES

Ann's story

I got a shock that night, I can tell you! You see, Mary had always been such a good girl – perhaps a bit outspoken sometimes. She used to go on a bit about the poor being downtrodden and the rich having too much... and when she got on to the rights of women – well – her Dad got annoyed about that. But she was no trouble, really. She had got engaged to Joe, the village carpenter when she was fifteen – and we thought – well – that marriage and a family would make her settle down.

But that night – shall I ever forget it! (Her Dad was out, thank the Lord). We were sitting sewing and she said quite calmly – "I'm expecting a baby, Mum".

I couldn't speak for a minute – Mary – my little girl – then I got angry "That Joe – your father will thrash him – and as for you – ".

""It's nothing to do with Joe", she said.

"Then – who -?"

"It was that day you went to see Aunt Hannah – this man walked in – ".

"You mean – he –".

"No, Mother – he said I would have a baby and that he would be the Son of God – and I said 'How – when I had never been with a man?' and he said it would happen through God's Holy Spirit and with God all things are possible".

I looked at her. I wondered if she had gone mad and was imagining all this – but she looked just as usual, except that she was serene – and sort of – radiant. I felt almost in awe of her... and then I pulled myself together. "Are you sure about this?" And she said "Yes, she was quite sure" – then I asked her "Does Joe know about it?"

"Oh, yes", she said "He was upset at first – said he wouldn't marry me because of the disgrace – but the angel came to him and told him it would be all right".

"That's all very well", I said. "But what are the neighbours going to say – they'll never believe what you've told me – and I don't know how I'm going to tell your Dad..."

"Poor Mum", she said gently. "If you like, I'll go and stay with Cousin Elizabeth for a bit – ".

And this she did. Joe took her there last week. But I can't help worrying about her.... and I do wonder – can her baby really be the one we've all been waiting for – the Messiah? The one who is going to change everything....?

Elizabeth's story

It was a shock – no doubt about that – I had given up all hope of having a baby, many years ago – and now Zach and I were old – and then – something strange happened to Zach, when it was his turn to burn the incense in the Temple (he's a priest, you know). When he came home he couldn't speak – I thought he might have had a stroke – but he seemed all right otherwise – and then he wrote me a note – “The Lord says we’re going to have a child”. I just laughed – thought his brain was turned – but – time went on – and I realised it was true – I was pregnant! I couldn’t believe it.....I didn’t go out for five months – the neighbours had been quite nasty about me not being able to have a baby – I wasn’t going to give them the chance to gossip now...

Then – who should walk in but my young cousin, Mary. “Can I come and stay with you, Liz?” she asked.

And as she spoke I felt my baby move within me – well – not only move – but jump, like he leaped for joy. And then I knew that Mary was pregnant like me, but that the baby she was carrying was even more special....Don’t ask me how I knew... I think that God told me... that Mary’s baby was the Holy One...God’s own Son..... I felt like bowing down to her.... I said to her, “You are the most blessed of all women, and blessed is the child you will have! Why should this great thing happen to me, that my Lord’s mother comes to visit me? For as soon as I heard your greeting the baby within me jumped for joy. How happy you are to believe that the Lord’s message to you will come true!”

Mary laughed – and cried – and came and hugged me- and then – started singing – “My soul magnifies the Lord...” It was like Hannah’s song that she sang when she knew that she had conceived and was carrying Samuel... and I had the feeling that this song would be sung for a very long time.... because Mary’s baby really is the one we’ve all been waiting for.... the Messiah.... and his coming would change the world.....

Anna's story

My name is Anna – I live in the Temple – have done since my husband died. I like it there, I've got a little room next to the broom cupboard and the people that sell the animals bring me the bit of food that I need. The priests don't mind, you see, because I do a bit of cleaning, sweep the floors and so on. I like it because I can pray there, and since my husband died I spend a lot of time talking to God – and listening to Him.

There's a lot going on in the Temple, a lot to see. There's this old man Simeon – well – I'm old but he looked like Methuselah! He spent a lot of time in prayer, too –and do you know what he said? He said that God had promised him that he wouldn't die until he'd seen the Messiah! Well – I didn't like to say so, but I thought it was wishful thinking - why should Simeon see him now?

But – I was wrong! That day, that special day, started like any other – pilgrims coming in, people in and out - it was dirty, wet weather and they didn't all wipe their feet on the door mat, drat them! Then a young couple came in with a baby –I thought, just another set of parents offering their first-born to the Lord.... but there was something different about this family. The mother was very young – she had a beautiful face with a sort of serene, steadfast look about her... her man was older, very protective of her and the child.... and the baby – he was beautiful! He couldn't have been more than four weeks old – but he held his little head up, he looked around him as though he knew the place and he smiled at everyone.

And then- there was old Simeon – he went right up to this young family, his face alight with joy. He actually took the baby from the mother and cuddled him! I was horrified – Simeon was so shaky I was afraid that he might drop him! But no – his grasp was firm and the little one laughed up at him and Simeon started praising God and saying "Lord, I'm ready to die now – I've seen him – the salvation of Israel – a light to lighten everyone!" And then he went on talking to the mother... and when I looked at Simeon's radiant face and that beautiful little boy in his arms I KNEW – that Simeon was right – it was TRUE - that God had sent a Saviour – his own Son! I praised God – I was so overflowing with joy that I just had to go out and tell everyone about it – because I KNEW - that this tiny baby was going to change the world.

ND - #0268 - 080726 - C0 - 197/132/6 - PB - 9781784561758 - Gloss Lamination